Fit for nothing

Howard Firkin
(that's not him ↑)

in case of emergency press

We are proud to acknowledge the Traditional Owners of country throughout Australia and to recognise their continuing connection to land, waters, and culture.

We pay our respects to their Elders past, present, and emerging.

We support recognition, reconciliation, and reparation.

Fit for nothing

Howard Firkin

in case of emergency press
http://www.icoe.com.au
Travancore, Victoria
Australia

Published by in case of emergency press 2015

Copyright © Howard Firkin 2015

All rights reserved. Without limiting the rights under copyright reserved above, no part of this publication may be reproduced, stored in or introduced into a database and retrieval system or transmitted in any form or any means (electronic, mechanical, photocopying, recording or otherwise) without the prior written permission of both the owner of copyright and the above publishers.

ISBN 978-0-9808304-9-1

"Islam is a Jewish conspiracy. The International Jewish Textile Conspiracy. It's all revealed in 2174. Wealthy Jewish textile moguls used Islam to increase sales of their fabrics. They were behind it from the start. Now, we're all clothed like this..."

Anne Hathaway

Table of contents

ACT 1 — 1
Scene 1	Ghost Dance	1
Scene 2	Victor Helot	1
Scene 3	Ghost 1 – Martin Heidegger	2
Scene 4	Ghost 2 – Anne Hathaway (Actor)	4
Scene 5	Ghost 3 – Anne Hathaway (WS)	6
Scene 6	Ghost Dance II	10

ACT 2 — 11
Scene 1	Mira Miswend	11
Scene 2	Spirit of the Keyboard	12
Scene 3	Spirit of the Office Chair	14
Scene 4	Spirit of the Music Keyboard	16
Scene 5	Spirit of the Times	17
Scene 6	Ghost Dance III	20

ACT III — 21
Scene 1	Joining the gym	21
Scene 2	Advice from the spirit world	24
Scene 3	Not joining the gym	25
Scene 4	Agreeing to fall in love	27
Scene 5	Love in the Age of Pish	28
Scene 6	Ghost Dance IV	31

ACT IV — 32
Scene 1	Advice from another age	32
Scene 2	He falls for her	34
Scene 3	She falls for him	36
Scene 4	Battle of the bands	37
Scene 5	It isn't going to work	40
Scene 6	Ghost Dance V	41

Act 1

Scene 1   Ghost Dance

MUSIC: "YOU'VE GOTTA GET UP AND DANCE" BY SUPERCHARGE (1977) STARTS. NO ONE LISTENS TO THIS ANYMORE SO IT SHOULD BE CHEAP TO LICENCE. SEE http://www.youtube.com/watch?v=Jm_xCjjoVMI

THREE GHOSTS BOOGIE ON AND DO A LITTLE LINE DANCE TO THE MUSIC. MUSIC FADES AND STOPS AT 0:56.

THE GHOSTS ARE THREE ACTORS WITH WHITE SHEETS OVER THEM; THE LESS CONVINCING THE BETTER. ONE GHOST MAY HAVE A SMALL BLACK MOUSTACHE PAINTED ON THE FACE.

THE GHOSTS BOW AND WITHDRAW.

Scene 2   Victor Helot

VICTOR ENTERS.

VICTOR   It's time I got fit.

I'm going to find a gym, pay far too much money to join it, and then I'm going to start going to the gym.

If I don't pay, I won't go; so I'm just going to bite the bullet and fork out the money. Whatever they ask for, I'm going to pay.

Look at me. I'm somewhere between thirty-five and forty, depending on who's playing me, and I'm flabby. No matter who's playing me, I'm flabby. I'm out of shape.

"No wonder he can't find a girlfriend," you're thinking. "He's out of shape."

You're right. On both counts. I can't find a girlfriend and I'm also out of shape. And I'm not getting any younger. So it's time to get fit. Pump iron. Run on a treadmill. Take a spin class. Use those funny stair climber things. Show the ex what she's missing out on. (*LIFTS HIS SHIRT TO*

EXPOSE HIS BELLY. CONSIDERS IT BRIEFLY…) Get some abs and then show her.

Look, I'm not a superficial man. You're probably thinking, "He's not going to stick at it! He's doing it for all the wrong reasons and he won't stick it out."

Well, you're wrong. I'm not a superficial man. I'm doing it for the right reasons. I want to be young forever and I want to be irresistible to women. Forever.

If that's the wrong reason, well, I'd like to hear the right reason.

Scene 3   Ghost 1 – Martin Heidegger

OFF STAGE GHOST 1 IS HEARD.

GHOST 1 IS THE GHOST OF MARTIN HEIDEGGER. IF WANTED, HIS SHEET CAN HAVE A SMALL BLACK MOUSTACHE PAINTED ON IT.

GHOST 1	Wooooo! Wooooo!

GHOST 1 ENTERS

	Wooooo! Good afternoon.
VICTOR	Hello. Who are you?
GHOST 1	I am Martin Heidegger. Ghost of.
VICTOR	Who? Or should I ask, "Whoooooooooo?"
GHOST 1	Don't be childish. I am Mart… I am the ghost of Martin Heidegger.
VICTOR	Am I supposed to know you?
GHOST 1	Know me? Wikipedia only says I'm "one of the most original and important philosophers of the 20th century".
VICTOR	Oh, yeah. The Nazi.
GHOST 1	(*SIGHS*) I was a member of the National Socialist Party, that's true.
VICTOR	And wrote a speech entitled "Declaration of Support for Adolf Hitler and the National Socialist State".

Act 1　　　　　　　　Scene 3　　　　　Ghost 1 – Martin Heidegger

GHOST 1　　For someone who didn't recognise my name, you're pretty good with the detail...

VICTOR　　Two can play the Wikipedia game.

GHOST 1　　All right. I wrote some regrettable speeches in the early thirties. By 1934 I had also resigned as rector of my university; my speeches were banned by the Party; I was under investigation by the Gestapo; and by 1944 I was elected "most expendable member of the faculty" and sent to dig trenches along the Rhine!

VICTOR　　Boo hoo. Everyone feels sorry for the Nazi. What can I do for you Marty? Why are you here?

GHOST 1　　The right reason.

VICTOR　　Not with you, old boy.

GHOST 1　　The right reason. You said you wanted to hear the right reason.

PAUSE. GHOST 1 LOOKS EXPECTANTLY AT VICTOR; VICTOR JUST LOOKS BLANK.

　　　　　　You said, "I want to be young forever and I want to be irresistible to women. If that's the wrong reason, well, I'd like to hear the right reason."

　　　　　　How are you doing this if you don't remember the script?

VICTOR　　I just make it up. But okay, let's hear the right reason. The *far* right reason, I expect...

GHOST 1　　The *right* reason has nothing to do with women or trying to cling to your youthful physique (*LOOKING DOUBTFULLY AT VICTOR*) but with being true to yourself and your destiny.

VICTOR　　My destiny? I'm a little light on for a destiny, I'm afraid. I just want to tone up, lose a bit of weight, meet a hot woman...

GHOST 1　　And that's the wrong reason. If you were doing this because you were impelled by an inner desire, by the unquenchable force of an inner will, by a burning desire to impose yourself and your physical presence, to reach new heights of corporeal excellence, then, and only then would this be worthwhile.

As it is, you are simply filling in time. Vacantly.

GHOST 1 EXITS

Woooooo!

Scene 4   Ghost 2 – Anne Hathaway (Actor)

VICTOR   That's ridiculous. Destiny. Who believes in destiny these days? Who can believe in it?

GHOST 2 IS HEARD OFF STAGE.

GHOST 2   Woooooo! Woooooo! I can!

GHOST 2 ENTERS

VICTOR   You can believe in destiny?

GHOST 2   Of course. I engineered my destiny.

VICTOR   Who are you?

GHOST 2   I am the ghost of Anne Hathaway.

VICTOR   Anne Hathaway? Shakespeare's wife?

GHOST 2   No. The actor. Big eyes, pretty, played in lots of movies in the late twentieth and early twenty-first centuries.

VICTOR   But she isn't dead yet! How can you be her ghost?

GHOST 2   This is two hundred years from now. The first time the great man's early plays are performed is nearly a hundred and seventy years after my death. I am well dead.

VICTOR   The great man? Do you mean Firkin's plays are being performed two hundred years from now? In 2214?

GHOST 2   No. Les Murray's plays are being performed. The play's been attributed to Les Murray for over a century. Audiences love Les Murray.

VICTOR   Yes, but he didn't write this play.

GHOST 2   He did now.

VICTOR	Hold on. If you're Anne Hathaway, show me your face.
GHOST 2	Can't. I'm a ghost. We all have to dress like this now.
VICTOR	Now?
GHOST 2	Yes. Now. 2214.
VICTOR	I'm lost. Why do ghosts have to dress like this now?
GHOST 2	Islam.
VICTOR	Islam? Islam has a dress code for ghosts?
GHOST 2	Yes. Islam. Islam has a dress code for everyone. It turned out they weren't hard-working, decent family types who were just trying to give their families a better life. It was all a gigantic conspiracy. They took over Australia. They took over the whole world.
VICTOR	A conspiracy? Who was behind it? Al-Quaeda? The House of Saud? The Iranians?
GHOST 2	The Jews. Islam is a Jewish conspiracy. The International Jewish Textile Conspiracy. It's all revealed in 2174. Wealthy Jewish textile moguls used Islam to increase sales of their fabrics. They were behind it from the start. Now, we're all clothed like this. By order of the Grand Mufti of the Planet, Moshe Goldberg.
VICTOR	I don't know what to say, Anne.
GHOST 2	Ask me a question.
VICTOR	Show us your face.
GHOST 2	I'll thank you to respect my religious choices, infidel.
VICTOR	Sorry. Okay, why do you make the films you do? And do you think they're any good?
GHOST 2	What's that supposed to mean?
VICTOR	Well, you know, you're beautiful, a good actor, but are your films worthy? When you look back on your achievements, are you happy? Or do you wish you'd made... I don't know... better films?

Act 1 Scene 5 *Ghost 3 – Anne Hathaway (WS)*

GHOST 2	Put it this way, son. I look back on my achievements and I think, "Well, at least I did something." And, by the way, I got very fit. A minor, a very minor, achievement in my life, but still a big, fat failure in yours.
VICTOR	No need to get personal. I wasn't trying to insult you. I just wanted to know was being famous and wealthy enough for you?
GHOST 2	And beautiful.
VICTOR	And beautiful. Was being famous and wealthy and beautiful enough for you?
GHOST 2	And talented.
VICTOR	All right, and talented. Was it enough?
GHOST 2	Well, it doesn't matter now, of course, but it mattered then.
VICTOR	And why doesn't it matter now? And why did it then?
GHOST 2	Well, it mattered then because I wanted it to matter. And it doesn't matter now because I'm dead. And obviously, nothing matters to me now, but the important point, Victor, is that I made it matter, so it did. Woooooo!

GHOST 2 MAKES TO LEAVE.

VICTOR	Anne, wait a minute!
GHOST 2	Yes?
VICTOR	Why do you all go 'Woooooo!' when you come and go?
GHOST 2	Some things are unchangeable. Inconsequential, meaningless, but unalterable. We have to wooooooo. There are things you have to do, too. You just don't know about them. Wooooooooooooooooo! (*EXITS*)

Scene 5   Ghost 3 – Anne Hathaway (WS)

VICTOR	Weird. I don't know what you're smoking in 2214, but it's working!

GHOST 3	(*OFF STAGE*) Wooooooo! Wooooooo!
GHOST 3 ENTERS	
	Nothing weird about it. I'd call it trite, a truism.
VICTOR	What's trite? And who are you?
GHOST 3	I am the ghost of Anne Hathaway.
VICTOR	Again? You sound different.
GHOST 3	I am different, idiot. I'm not that actress trollop.
VICTOR	Oh? You're the other Anne Hathaway.
GHOST 3	No. I'm not the other Anne Hathaway, I'm the *real* Anne Hathaway.
VICTOR	Hardly real...
GHOST 3	You know what I mean.
VICTOR	… and not a trollop, obviously, although you did marry Will in a hurry and have a baby pretty damn quick afterwards.
GHOST 3	Enough! Different times. Less sanctimonious nonsense, in my day. Now, before I hie me hence, you may ask me any question you like. Anything at all. Even a question about the big man, if you like. I'll answer you anything. But only one question. One question is all you get. Think carefully.
VICTOR	And then you hie yourself hence? (*QUICKLY*) That's not a question!
GHOST 3	Okay. One question.
VICTOR	Let's think… You married William Shakespeare when he was eighteen and you were twenty-six. That's pretty unusual. What was the reason for that, Anne?
GHOST 3	The reason? The reason is that I was born eight years before he was. Stupid question. I'm hieing off.
GHOST 3 MAKES TO LEAVE STAGE	
VICTOR	No! Wait!
GHOST 3 TURNS BACK	

GHOST 3	Only fooling! All that 'only one question' malarkey... just to fool you. Make a cat laugh to see how the Shakespeare scholars sweat when I tell them they've got just one question!
VICTOR	Why are you here? I'm no scholar. I'm just working out whether or not to join a gym and get fit.
GHOST 3	Destiny.
VICTOR	Destiny again? What's destiny got to do with it?
GHOST 3	Mind if I sit?
VICTOR	Oh, sure. (LOOKING AROUND BARE STAGE). But there's no chair.
GHOST 3	That's all right. Got my own.

GHOST 3 HAS A STOOL CONCEALED BENEATH THE SHEET AND SITS ON IT

	Destiny is the only thing. Look to destiny.
VICTOR	Look to destiny...
GHOST 3	What would I have been to you if I had married one of my other suitors?
VICTOR	You had others?
GHOST 3	Others! Beating them off with a stick, I was! If I wasn't forced to wear this damned sheet, you'd see something to put a tent in your lycra! Of course I had other suitors! I was still young. I was pretty. I had property. And... (CHUCKLES KNOWINGLY)
VICTOR	And?
GHOST 3	And, I was a really good fuck, Victor. I loved it. Get me on my back and get ready for an afternoon's entertainment!
VICTOR	Something I didn't need to know.
GHOST 3	Oh, lighten up. Still suffering from Victorian prudery all these centuries later. Let me tell you, boy, when the plague's in town, nobody's too worried about who's doing what to whom. Or what.
VICTOR	So, what was he like, Shakespeare?

Act 1   Scene 5   Ghost 3 – Anne Hathaway (WS)

GHOST 3   Oh, he was a good man for me. As a young man, he was serious. He knew what he wanted and he was going to get it. He needed a partner and so did I. We were made for each other.

VICTOR   But he left you to go to London. He was away for years.

GHOST 3   He left me to go to London and he made a lot of money and he was back and forth all the time! He was a hardworking man. That's why I picked him. I didn't need someone who was going to drink my property away and beat me when it was gone. I wanted a good man, a husband, and he was that. A good provider, my Will.

VICTOR   And what of his other loves? The Young Man, the Dark Lady?

GHOST 3   Ask yourself, smartarse, who did he return to? Who did he live with? Who warmed his bed from eighteen to death?

VICTOR   Did you know he was a great writer? Did you know we'd be reading him six hundred years after his death?

GHOST 3   Don't be stupid. He wrote to make money. To live. That's something else I taught him.

VICTOR   To make money?

GHOST 3   No, fool. How to write verse.

VICTOR   You taught him?

GHOST 3   The sweetest songs my garden birds can sing

             I gave to him. My lips, my tongue, my breath,

             were his to use to form those words which ring

             the world around, which mock the thought of death.

             That's pentameter, that is. Iamb a champ at it. I can knock it out by the yard. Easier than churning butter. Smoother, too. I taught him how to do it.

VICTOR   How?

Fit for nothing   9

GHOST 3	Stop thinking, Will, I told him. Stop *trying* all the time. Let it flow. Those fuckers in the audience won't know any better anyway. Just write it down!
VICTOR	Wow. Inspiring stuff, Anne.
GHOST 3	Get fucked. What've you done, that makes you so smug?
VICTOR	Hey! I didn't claim that I'd done anything…
GHOST 3	"I didn't claim…" Pathetic. No, you don't claim anything. You don't do anything. Destiny, mate. Look to destiny. And you want to know something about your future?
VICTOR	You can see the future?
GHOST 3	Yours, I can.
VICTOR	Well?
GHOST 3	You'll never get fit. See you round, buttered-arse. And I do mean round.

GHOST 3 STANDS, LEAVING THE STOOL BEHIND FOR THE FOLLOWING SCENE. LOOKS INTENTLY AT THE STOOL.

VICTOR	What are you doing?
GHOST 3	I always make a point of examining my stool.

GHOST 3 EXITS CACKLING AT OWN JOKE.

Scene 6   Ghost Dance II

MUSIC FADES IN FROM 0:49
GHOSTS BOOGIE ON AND CONTINUE THEIR DANCE.
MUSIC FADES AND STOPS AT 1:38.
GHOSTS BOW AND WITHDRAW.

Act 2

Scene 1   Mira Miswend

MIRA ENTERS AND VICTOR EXITS. THEY DO NOT ACKNOWLEDGE EACH OTHER. MIRA SEATS HERSELF ON THE STOOL AND MIMES OFFICE TASKS: TYPING, TELEPHONING, FILING.

MIRA   This is killing me. No, I mean it literally. This is killing me. Slowly… but killing me.

Stuck in this pointless job, sitting, settling, spreading like a jelly at a summer picnic. Spilling over the sides. Sticky, gooey, slippery.

This is killing me.

Stupid, idiotic, pointless job. To get enough money to buy food, rent a flat, buy the train tickets, come to work to earn enough money to buy food, rent a flat, buy a train ticket, come to work.

This is killing me.

And look. I'm getting fat. I'm getting fat because I spend all day on my arse serving these fuckers who ponce around in a gym because they haven't got any real work to keep them occupied.

And who am I to judge them? It's not like I've got a real job either. We're all just poncing around or sitting on our arses. No one's doing any real work at all.

This is not what I trained for. It's not what I thought I'd end up doing. At night, I still practice. I still work on my music, but this soul destroying work. This spiritless place.

MIRA RETURNS TO HER TYPING. AS SHE MIMES, THE SOUND OF A KEYBOARD TAPPING IS HEARD, MIXED WITH SOFT ETHEREAL MUSIC OFF STAGE WHICH GRADUALLY GROWS IN VOLUME.

Scene 2   Spirit of the Keyboard

MIRA CONTINUES TYPING BUT IS PUZZLED BY THE MUSIC. SPIRIT 1 DANCES ONTO STAGE. SPIRITS CAN REUSE THE SHEETS OF THE GHOSTS, BUT THEIR FACES ARE VISIBLE. MUSIC FADES AS THE SPIRIT DANCES TOWARDS MIRA. IN THE FOLLOWING, WHENEVER THE SPIRIT USES THE WORD 'SPIRIT' IT DANCES OR SPINS AROUND.

MIRA	Who are you?
SPIRIT 1	Liar.
MIRA	Lyre—like the harp thing? Or liar like the politician?
SPIRIT 1	Liar. You are a liar.
MIRA	Me?
SPIRIT 1	You. Liar.
MIRA	Who are you and what do you want? Why are you here?
SPIRIT 1	"Spiritless place". You said this was a spiritless place, but you are wrong. I am a spirit. I am in this place.
MIRA	You're a spirit?
SPIRIT 1	Yes, I am the Spirit of the Keyboard.
MIRA	Keyboard? Keyboards have spirits?
SPIRIT 1	A spirit. Not plural. Singular. A. A spirit. Me. The Spirit of the Keyboard. Eternal and beautiful. The Spirit of the Keyboard.
MIRA	Eternal and beautiful. If you're eternal, what were you doing before keyboards were invented?
SPIRIT 1	Dark days, Mira. Dark, long days.
MIRA	Well, we're all trapped and tapping along now. Shouldn't you be tap dancing?
SPIRIT 1	Very amusing. Ask.
MIRA	Ask what?
SPIRIT 1	Ask me your question. Not that one.
MIRA	This is very confusing. My question?
SPIRIT 1	Your question. Ask.

Act 2 *Scene 2* *Spirit of the Keyboard*

MIRA What are you doing here?
SPIRIT 1 Not that question. Ask.
MIRA What am I doing here?
SPIRIT 1 That's it!

SPIRIT MUSIC STARTS AGAIN AND THE SPIRIT BEGINS AN ELABORATE DANCE.

MIRA Stop! What are you doing?
SPIRIT 1 (*DISCOURAGED*) I thought it was obvious. I was answering your question.
MIRA Words, please.
SPIRIT 1 Very well. What you are doing here is celebrating.
MIRA Celebrating? I thought I was just complaining about how this stupid, pointless job was killing me!
SPIRIT 1 That is, indeed, what you were *saying*, but what you were *doing* was celebrating. Every little tap, tap, tap on your keyboard is the sacred chime of a musical bell, celebrating me, the Spirit of the Keyboard. You are offering me your obeisance and I thank you for it; I reward you for it.
MIRA How are you rewarding me?
SPIRIT 1 Like this!

SPIRIT MUSIC STARTS AND THE SPIRIT RECOMMENCES ITS ELABORATE DANCE.

MIRA Stop! And stop that awful bloody music! Stop! I can't think straight.
SPIRIT 1 Well, I can stop allowing you to see me, to hear the music, but it won't stop me accepting your praise!
MIRA What are you talking about? Why should I care whether you think I'm praising you or not?
SPIRIT 1 Whether you care or not, is no concern of mine. That's for you to torture yourself with. All I'm explaining is that all work is its celebration. You don't need to know or understand it. That's up to you.
MIRA It's still bloody pointless.

SPIRIT 1	No, it isn't.
MIRA	Why am I doing this? What difference does it make to anyone? A monkey could do this job. If it had a big enough arse to sit on.
SPIRIT 1	They're actually not much good at sitting still, monkeys. But perhaps a well-trained golden retriever could do it.
MIRA	Well, this has been very helpful, but I've got lots of pointless work to do. Endless, repetitive, pointless work. Pointlessly round and round.

Scene 3   Spirit of the Office Chair

ETHEREAL SPIRIT MUSIC STARTS AGAIN.

SPIRIT 2	(*OFF STAGE*) Not true! Essential!

SPIRIT 2 DANCES ONTO STAGE.

MIRA	Goody. Another one. Who are you?
SPIRIT 2	I am the Spirit of the Office Chair.
MIRA	And what are you doing here? I've got work to do.
SPIRIT 2	I am here to offer correction.
MIRA	Yes?
SPIRIT 1	She doesn't take correction very well, but go ahead by all means.
SPIRIT 2	Round and round is not pointless. Round and round is essential. An essential element of my dance, of course, (*DEMONSTRATING*) but essential in any dance.
MIRA	What are you talking about?
SPIRIT 2	Office chairs spin round and round. You sit on one all day—nice arse, by the way—so you must have noticed. It isn't pointless, it's essential. And not just for chairs, but everyone, everything. Everything is spinning. Everything. The sun, the earth, the moon, everything. Every atom in your body spins. We spin. You spin. Everything is spinning round and round. No spin, no dance. We spin when we dance.

THE SPIRITS DEMONSTRATE

MIRA	Fine! We're spinning. It was an expression. An expression of frustration. Getting nowhere, you know? Spinning round and round and getting nowhere.
SPIRIT 2	(*TO SPIRIT 1*) Not too bright, this one. (*TO MIRA*) All right, dear. Let's go through this together, shall we?
	Spinning round and round and getting nowhere. All right. Currently, you're nowhere, apparently. So are we. And you'd like to get somewhere, would you?
MIRA	I'm speaking figuratively.
SPIRIT 2	Clever thing. Figuratively, then. You'd like to be somewhere.
MIRA	Figuratively, yes.
SPIRIT 2	Where? Figuratively.
MIRA	I don't know! I just don't want to be stuck doing this when I could be doing something useful, something I want to do with my life.
SPIRIT 2	Ah! Now I see. Now, I can tell you what you should be doing.
MIRA	You can?
SPIRIT 2	(*IRRITATEDLY*) No, of course I can't! Foolish girl. "I want to do something". Something isn't anything, it's nothing, it's just a word. Something is nothing until you make it something. No one says, "I want to do nothing with my life!", but that's what you're saying.
	"I want to do something!" What's the 'something', woman?
MIRA	I don't know! Perhaps something to do with music. I like playing music.

Scene 4   Spirit of the Music Keyboard

DISCORDANT MUSIC STARTS—SOME SORT OF AVANT GARDE JAZZ WITH SOMEONE FARTING INTO A TRUMPET OR SOMETHING. SPIRIT 3 DANCES ON IN AN ERRATIC, SPASMODIC, ARHYTHMIC DANCE.

SPIRIT 1	Great. She mentions music. (*NODS TO SPIRIT 3*) Miles.
SPIRIT 2	(*ALSO ACKNOWLEDGING SPIRIT 3*) Miles.
SPIRIT 3	Guys! Great to see you.
MIRA	Miles? Who are you?
SPIRIT 3	I am the Spirit of the Keyboard.
MIRA	I thought there was only one of those.
SPIRIT 1	The other sort of keyboard. Music keyboard.
MIRA	(*IMPRESSED*) Oh! And why 'Miles'?
SPIRIT 2	That's how far away everyone else wants to be.
SPIRIT 3	He's joking! No, it's a homage.
MIRA	Miles Davis?
SPIRIT 3	The man!
SPIRIT 2	So, you've come for a reason, Miles?
SPIRIT 3	Yes, the reason. She said, she'd like to be playing music.
MIRA	Yes, instead of this pointless job, I'd like to be home, working on my music.
SPIRIT 3	Which would be, like, so cool, except for one thing.
MIRA	Which is?
SPIRIT 3	Which is… you're lying.
SPIRIT 1	Don't bother. I've already told her she's a liar.
MIRA	What do you mean, lying? And how do you know?
SPIRIT 3	Because, my dear, if you weren't lying, you'd be home right now, playing, writing, listening. And you're not. You're here.
MIRA	I'm here, arsehole, because I have to eat.

SPIRIT 3	That's true, but you're not eating. And you're not playing music. So what are you doing here?
MIRA	I'm earning money!
SPIRIT 3	Yes, you are. But here's a tip. If you want to play music, play. You won't starve. Or you may starve a bit. But you won't die. Or you may die eventually, but you'll make music before you die.
	Keep working here, and you'll still die. But you won't be making any music, baby.
MIRA	Listen! It's easy enough for you to say. It's easy for anyone to say. I still have to make enough money to live. I have to live somewhere. I have to pay to live somewhere. I have to eat. I have to pay to have something to eat.
	The only people who are free to make music all day are people who have been lucky enough to be discovered or who happen to write the sort of crap that gets played on the radio now.
	And that's not me. I'm not that good or that bad. But why should I have to be stuck here doing this? I don't want to be fabulously rich or even famous. I just want to do what I'm good at and be able to live in these squalid, ridiculous, spiritually impoverished times.

ALL THE SPIRITS SCURRY OFF STAGE, ALARMED.

Scene 5   Spirit of the Times

MUSIC OFF STAGE—HEAVIER, MORE OMINOUS THAN PREVIOUS SPIRIT MUSIC. SPIRIT 4 DANCES ONTO THE STAGE IN A STATELY, HEAVY-FOOTED, PRECISE DANCE.

MIRA	Who are you? I take it by the way you've scared off all the others that you're some sort of big wheel in the spirit world.
SPIRIT 4	The biggest. I am Pish, the Spirit of the Age.
MIRA	What age?
SPIRIT 4	This age. Now.
MIRA	This is the Age of Pish?

SPIRIT 4	No, although you may wish to call it that, but technically, Pish is *my* name. The Age doesn't have a name. It's not Golden or Dark or Enlightened or anything; so it doesn't have a name.
MIRA	Not much of an Age, then?
SPIRIT 4	No, but it's mine. And, as it happens, yours, too. And I'm the Spirit of it. With my help, you could become one of the great ones of this Age.
MIRA	What's the point if it's such a lousy age anyway?
SPIRIT 4	Oh, hark at her! "Such a lousy age…"! What's it to you, lady? Do you think you're going to get to live in another age? Do you think you'll even get to see another age?
MIRA	No, probably not.
SPIRIT 4	No probably about it, honey. This is it for you. Like or lump it.
MIRA	All right! It's the only age I've got. What are you doing here, anyway, Pish. Haven't you got more important things to be doing?
SPIRIT 4	Of course. At least, many things… several things as important…
	But I'm here to advise you. You said you wanted to know how to do what you're good at and be able to live in these times. Well, I can tell you.
MIRA	Tell me what?
SPIRIT 4	How to do it. How to be one of the great ones of the age. How to be admired, respected, *paid* in this Age of Pish.
MIRA	But I don't want to be "one of the great ones". I'm not. I know I'm not. I'm okay. My music is okay. It's not great, but it's better than most, and it's still worth something, even if it isn't great. I just wish I'd been born into an age when music was appreciated.
SPIRIT 4	And what good would that have done you? You would have been recognised as the mediocre talent you are. You should be grateful to be living

	in the Age of Pish. It's much easier to be one of the great ones in an ordinary age than in a great one. Anyone can do it.
MIRA	Anyone?
SPIRIT 4	Anyone.
MIRA	Anyone with a bit more than a mediocre talent.
SPIRIT 4	No. Anyone. [*SLYLY*] Anyone moved by the Spirit of the Age, that is.
MIRA	And what does that involve?
SPIRIT 4	Generally, it involves sacrifice. Sacrifice and hard work. And dedication. And a piece of tail every now and then.
MIRA	What?
SPIRIT 4	Come on. No games with me. You can't expect something for nothing. Not these days. And if the Spirit of the Office Chair thinks you've got a cute arse, that's good enough for me. He sees a lot, you know.
MIRA	Fuck off, creep! I thought you were a spirit? How could you even... even do anything?
SPIRIT 4	Oh, I don't know. I thought I'd try it. It's a compliment, really. I know you're worried about it, but your arse isn't too big. It's nice. And I just thought, you know, we could...
MIRA	Ergh. Forget it, Pish.
	So that's the Spirit of the Age. Everybody's out to get a bit, even if they're incapable. Thanks for your help and concern, but I've got work to do now.
SPIRIT 4	At least think about it.
MIRA	You know what, Pish? I think I'll pass. I'll try waiting for a new age.
SPIRIT 4	You'll be waiting a while! Two hundred years from now, I'm still appearing as the Spirit of the Age!
MIRA	Yeah, but so am I. Thanks, but no thanks.
SPIRIT 4	Frigid bitch. I blame Uzlamb for this.

MIRA	What? What's "Uzlam"?
SPIRIT 4	Uzlamb. With a "b" on the end. You know, a hundred years after this was written, Australia was invaded and ceased to exist.
MIRA	What?
SPIRIT 4	Yes, Tony Abbott was right and very, very wrong. While everyone was worried about boats from the west, the threat was all from the east. A radical form of Islam developed in New Zealand: Uzlamb. In many ways, a confusing religion. They invaded; Australia lost. They used to write the "U" so it looked like an "N". Their marketing was very slick. Appealed to the young men.
MIRA	Pish?
SPIRIT 4	Yes?
MIRA	Fuck off.

MIRA AND SPIRIT 4 EXIT IN DIFFERENT DIRECTIONS.

Scene 6   Ghost Dance III

MUSIC FADES IN FROM 1:30.
GHOSTS BOOGIE ON AND CONTINUE THEIR DANCE.
MUSIC FADES AND STOPS AT 2:25.
GHOSTS BOW AND WITHDRAW.

Act III

Scene 1   Joining the gym

MIRA IS SEATED ON THE STOOL MIMING HER OFFICE ACTIVITIES FACING ONE SIDE OF THE STAGE. VICTOR ENTERS FROM THE SIDE MIRA IS FACING AND WALKS DIFFIDENTLY OVER TO HER. ALL THE OFFICE ACTIVITIES OF BOTH MIRA AND VICTOR ARE MIMED.

MIRA   (*GIVING GOOD RECEPTION*) Good morning, sir. How can I help you?

VICTOR   I've come to join the gym.

MIRA   Excellent! Has anyone explained the packages available to you?

VICTOR   No. This is my first time here. Or any gym, actually.

MIRA   (*FLIRTING PROFESSIONALLY*) Hard to believe. You look in pretty good shape to me.

VICTOR   Really? I thought I was getting flabby. Starting to look like the sedentary slob I am.

MIRA   Well, we can all stand improvement, can't we? That's why we're here.

Now, at *Fit For Living Life* we offer a completely personalised service where the level of membership and access to services is completely customisable and packaged to meet your individual needs.

To start us off, all we need to do is get you to fill out this questionnaire, and that will give us an indication of the level of membership which will suit you best.

HANDS HIM A FORM.

VICTOR   Great. How much does it cost?

MIRA   *Fit For Living Life* isn't like other gyms. Our packages are customised to suit the individual to ensure a maximal benefit-outcome-to-investment ratio. It's all explained in the form.

VICTOR   And what does that come to? Typically.

Act III   *Scene 1*   *Joining the gym*

MIRA   Are you a 'typical' gym member?

VICTOR   If your typical gym members are sedentary slobs, I am.

MIRA   Let's see… (SCROLLING THROUGH A SCREEN DISPLAY)… no, no 'Sedentary Slob' package, I'm afraid. How about you try filling in the questionnaire?

VICTOR MOVES AWAY TO A CORNER OF THE OFFICE AND BEGINS TO FILL IN THE QUESTIONNAIRE.

VICTOR   Why do you need to know my occupation?

MIRA   Gives us an indication of how much physical activity you do in your working life. You can leave it blank if you like.

VICTOR   You don't charge more if I say I'm a dentist?

MIRA   Are you?

VICTOR   No.

MIRA   Just fill in the form.

VICTOR CONTINUES FILLING IN THE FORM.

VICTOR   Medical history. I've never heard of some of these things!

MIRA   That means you haven't got them, then.

VICTOR   (FEELING HIS STOMACH GINGERLY) But I might have. What's a gastric ulcer feel like?

MIRA   Like being stabbed in the stomach by an angry girlfriend.

VICTOR   I haven't got a girlfriend.

MIRA   Well, there's a surprise.

VICTOR   Not really cut out for this job, are you?

MIRA   Sorry. I've been thinking the same thing myself.

          Look, this gym is just like every other gym. Our prices are almost identical to everyone else's because they have to be. The only thing we offer that's not advertised is that we'll give you a special deal on your first year's membership if you switch from another gym.

Act III   Scene 1   Joining the gym

	We don't advertise it, because everyone would just say they're from another gym, but if you want to tell me that, I'll give you the discount.
VICTOR	Okay. But I've never been in another gym.
MIRA	And if you want the discount, now would be the time to stop telling me.
VICTOR	Right. So how much will it cost me with the discount?
MIRA	Annual or monthly?
VICTOR	Annual. I'd rather get the pain over fast. And I'm not going to get fit in a month.
MIRA	Do you want access to classes or just the machines?
VICTOR	What do you recommend?
MIRA	Me? I get a commission on every person I sign up. Do you really want my recommendation?
VICTOR	What would you recommend to a friend?
MIRA	To a friend, I'd recommend saving their money. To you, annual membership, full access.
VICTOR	Do you go to the gym?
MIRA	Four days a week, without fail. I work here, friend.
VICTOR	No, I meant, Do you work out at a gym? You look sort of sporty.
MIRA	No I don't work out. And I'm not sporty. I'm just too poor to overeat.
VICTOR	So you'd welcome an invitation to come out to lunch some time?
MIRA	Probably not that poor. Sorry.
VICTOR	That's okay. Knock backs are not an unknown in my life. I wouldn't have known where to take you anyway.
MIRA	Think you'll complete the questionnaire for me?
VICTOR	Doesn't seem much point, does it?
MIRA	What about getting fit?
VICTOR	Yeah. How many of the people who sign up ever get fit, or change their lives?

Fit for nothing   23

MIRA	About a third. A quarter? Or less… Say, one in five.
VICTOR	I'm not that remarkable.
MIRA	Wow. Neither am I, but I hope I wouldn't think one in five was too exclusive.
VICTOR	Yeah, well, long experience. Thanks for the advice. I'll think about it.
MIRA	Okay. Let me know.
VICTOR	See you.
MIRA	Yep. See you round.

EXIT VICTOR. MIRA RETURNS TO HER OFFICE FUNCTIONS.

Scene 2   Advice from the spirit world

ETHEREAL MUSIC STARTS OFF STAGE.

MIRA	Oh great. They're back.
SPIRIT 2	(*OFF STAGE*) Just me. (*SPIRIT 2 DANCES ON*) Just me.
MIRA	Office chair, right?
SPIRIT 2	Spirit of the Office Chair, correct.
MIRA	Why are you back. To offer more corrections?
SPIRIT 2	No, no. Congratulations. Just to offer congratulations. And perhaps some advice.
MIRA	Congratulations for what?
SPIRIT 2	For the beautiful, one might almost say spiritual, technique you employed to spin him around. You know my thoughts on spinning. Beautiful job. And on yourself.
MIRA	On myself?
SPIRIT 2	Yes. The way you spin yourself around. On the axis of your sphincter. Beautiful to watch.
MIRA	What are you talking about?
SPIRIT 2	You are attracted to the gormless one, but you spin yourself around and reject him. An office chair couldn't have done it better.

MIRA	Attracted to him? What are you talking about? He's pudgy and unfit and not even a dentist.
SPIRIT 2	(*DANCING OFF STAGE*) And yet, and yet, and yet…

SPIRIT 2 EXITS. MIRA RETURNS TO HER TASKS DISCONSOLATELY.

MIRA	(*CALLS OFF STAGE*) Hey! You said you had some advice! (*EXITS*)

Scene 3   Not joining the gym

VICTOR ENTERS. STANDS BEFORE THE STOOL, WAITING. CHECKS HIS WATCH OCCASIONALLY. MIRA ENTERS.

MIRA	Sorry I'm late.

SETTLES HERSELF BEHIND HER DESK. SWITCHES ON HER COMPUTER. SHUFFLES SOME PAPERS.

	Sorry. How can I help?
VICTOR	Hi. I was in this morning?
MIRA	Of course, hi! You've decided to join?
VICTOR	No, I've decided not to join. I wanted to talk to you.
MIRA	About what?
VICTOR	About life. About what we're doing. About what I'm doing. About going out for lunch.
MIRA	That's very sweet, really, but I've just been to lunch and I have to work for the rest of the day. That's the deal. Pretty standard.
GHOST 1	(*OFF STAGE*) Wooooo! Wooooo!
MIRA	What did you say?
VICTOR	Oh good. At least you can hear him, too.

GHOST 1 ENTERS

GHOST 1	Wooooo! Idiot!
MIRA	What? Who are you? And why are you wearing a sheet?
GHOST 1	Islam. We've been through all that.
MIRA	Uzlamb?

GHOST 1	No, that was only in Australia and only for a few decades. Eventually all the kiwis went home. They always do in the end. This play opens in London. Islam.
VICTOR	He's a ghost.
MIRA	And what's he doing here?
GHOST 1	I'm here to help this idiot. He thinks he wants to ask you out, but he has bigger fish to fry.
MIRA	What's it to you if he asks me out?
GHOST 1	Nothing, nothing, nothing. But that's the point isn't it? Nothing. Waste of time. Fruitless activity for no purpose.
MIRA	Thanks a lot, mate.
VICTOR	What are the bigger fish?
MIRA	What do mean? Suddenly I'm not good enough for you, Mr One-In-Five?
VICTOR	No, no! Not at all! I just thought I should hear what he has to say about it. It's the first I've heard about bigger fish.
GHOST 1	We have spoken extensively about it, but you simply haven't understood.
VICTOR	Well, tell me now.
GHOST 1	Tell me now, tell me now. Who am I to be ordered around by you? You didn't even ask me here. I came by myself.
MIRA	He's touchy for a ghost, isn't he?
VICTOR	He used to be a professor. He's okay once you get used to him.
GHOST 1	Big of you. You are not here to ask this woman out. Stop pussyfooting around! You want to fuck her. You want to impregnate her. You want her to carry your stock and enrich it with her—frankly—superior genes.
MIRA	Whoa, cowboy! I don't even know his name!
VICTOR	Victor.
MIRA	Mira. Pleased to meet you, Victor, and thrilled to be asked to enrich your genetic stock.

GHOST 1		Get on with it, you two! Victor, you have a will. Start using it! Start exerting it! Without a will there is only Being. And Being is nothing. Demonstrably nothing. Look at me. Here I am, being. But a ghost, therefore, not being.
		Dasein, schmasein. Being is nothing. Take her!
VICTOR		There's a reason…
GHOST 1		(*CUTS HIM OFF AND RANTS*) Reason me no reason, you idiot! You fool! You think you can reason? With that thing you call a brain, you think you can reason? You haven't got the capacity to reason! That you try to reason is proof of that! Your attempts to reason are the deadliest enemies of reason! The best of the species can't reason consistently—and you think you'll be able to? Take her! Accept who and what you are. Take her! Action, not reason! Action!

GHOST 1 STORMS OFF STAGE. HURRIEDLY RETURNS TO MOAN.

Wooooo! Sorry. Forgot.

Scene 4   Agreeing to fall in love

VICTOR AND MIRA REMAIN ON STAGE

MIRA	Well. That was a bit awkward.
VICTOR	Yes, sorry about that.
MIRA	So who was your spooky friend in the sheet?
VICTOR	That's Heidegger. Martin Heidegger, the philosopher.
MIRA	Heidegger? Wasn't he a Nazi?
VICTOR	Yes, but only in an intellectual sense.
MIRA	An intellectual sense? He didn't kill Jews, he just thought about it?
VICTOR	No, well, perhaps, I don't know. He didn't believe in reason. At least, he believed in it, but he thought it was bad. And I think the lack of reason in National Socialism appealed to him.

	I've been trying to read his work a bit since I met him. It's… it's not always terribly clear.
MIRA	And he's the guy you've been taking advice from?
VICTOR	Yes. No! I mean, I haven't had much choice. He just turns up. I don't 'take advice from him'. But I do listen to him. Not that I have a lot of choice…
MIRA	That's okay. Unwelcome visitors are something we all have to deal with.
VICTOR	Meaning me? I can go.
MIRA	Lighten up, Victor. And work a bit. Fight a bit. Don't expect things handed to you on a plate. You want to ask me out? Ask!
VICTOR	Without suggesting that you bear my children, would you like to go out with me some time?
MIRA	Okay. I've sort of boxed myself into it, haven't I?
VICTOR	Great. I'll call you here before you knock off tonight.
MIRA	That would be nice. Talk later, Victor.

EXIT VICTOR.

Scene 5   Love in the Age of Pish

THE PORTENTOUS SPIRIT MUSIC SOUNDS.

MIRA	Again the music! I have to work!

SPIRIT 4 DANCES ON CAUTIOUSLY.

SPIRIT 4	Has that idiot gone?
MIRA	You know Victor?
SPIRIT 4	Not that idiot. The other one. Heidegger. Has he gone?
MIRA	Yes, he's gone. Why? You don't like him?
SPIRIT 4	Don't like him? Who cares about him? Mere ghost. He's nothing to me. I just prefer not to associate with him. Old windbag.
MIRA	What have you got against him, Pish?

SPIRIT 4	It's more the other way around. He's not too keen on me. Classic case of mistaking cause and effect, but you can't tell him. He won't listen to reason.
MIRA	Okay. What's he got against you?
SPIRIT 4	He blames me for the age. I keep telling him, it's my age, but I'm not responsible for it. I'm just the spirit of it. The age is made by those living in it—they're responsible for me, not the other way around.
MIRA	What's he got against the age?
SPIRIT 4	You need to ask? The thousand year Reich fell nine hundred and eighty seven years short of target. He blames the age.

He had high hopes for the Reich, you know. He knew it was run by idiots, but that's why he thought it would succeed. He's been disappointed ever since. |
MIRA	Well, he's gone and I'm not interested. What can I do for you before you leave?
SPIRIT 4	I was just going to offer you some help.
MIRA	I'd hoped I'd made it clear that I want none of your help, Pish. And I'm certainly not interested in paying for it.
SPIRIT 4	You misunderstand me. My previous words may have been taken out of context. Leave aside your mistaken personal interpretation of my words and allow me to clarify my function.
MIRA	Clarify away, Pish, but keep your hands to yourself, okay?
SPIRIT 4	The Spirit of the Age is the moving spirit of the times. It inseminates every action of the age. I'm here to ensure success in your coming action.
MIRA	Oh, yes? And this insemination you're contemplating…
SPIRIT 4	Poor choice of words. I'm here to help. You want to fall in love. You want him to fall in love. I can do that. Spirit of the Age. All part of my brief.

MIRA	What are you talking about? Love? Who mentioned love? One poor, sedentary slob has asked me out for a date, or lunch, or something. No one's thinking about love, Pish.
SPIRIT 4	Pish, indeed. Of course you're both thinking about love. What else is there to think about? Lunch? I know the age is obsessed with trivial things, but not even you people are that shallow.
MIRA	Too fast. Way too fast, Pish. Love? I've got other things to think about, and Victor, too, probably.
SPIRIT 4	Ask him.
MIRA	What?
SPIRIT 4	Ask him. Ask him if he'd like to fall in love. You can explain that I'll take care of it. Ask him when... (*PISH WAITS EXPECTANTLY FOR A COUPLE OF SECONDS*)

SOUND OF A TELEPHONE RINGING

... when he calls you.

MIRA MIMES ANSWERING THE PHONE

MIRA	*Fit For Living Life*, the gym that's different because you are. You're speaking to Mira, how can I help?
	Oh, hi. How're you? Still willing to take a chance on lunch?
	Okay. No, that's fine. That works for me. Dinner sounds good. I finish here at 5:30. I can meet you there around 7:00 for a drink.
	Sure.
	Okay.

PISH COUGHS SIGNIFICANTLY

Yep. Okay.

There's one other thing. I'll explain when we meet, but remember the little contretemps with Heidegger?

No, no, it's okay. I've sort of got one of my own.

No, a spirit.

	A spirit. It's different, apparently. Touchy in a different way. He's Pish, the Spirit of the Age. Quite a big deal in the spirit world, if one believes him.
	Yes. Anyway, I'll explain—as much as I can—later, but he's asked me to ask you a question.
	How do you feel about falling in love?
SPIRIT 4	No. Do you want to fall in love?
MIRA	Sorry. No. Do you want to fall in love?
	Yes.
	Yes, that's what he asked. He can do it, apparently.
	Who knows? He says he can.
	Okay. (*TURNING TO PISH*) He says, "Okay".
SPIRIT 4	Okay? Just 'Okay'? This is the Age I'm given…
MIRA	Okay. See you tonight.
SHE HANGS UP.	
	Okay. We're on. Love it is. I have work to do now.
SPIRIT 4	I'm offering love! I'm offering to make you and Victor a pair, a name, one of the great loves of the Age!
MIRA	And thanks. But I have to finish the customer retention reports for the month. It's considered important in your age.

EXIT SPIRIT 4 TO PORTENTOUS MUSIC. MIRA MIMES WORKING FOR A FEW MOMENTS THEN EXITS, TAKING THE STOOL.

Scene 6   Ghost Dance IV

MUSIC FADES IN FROM 2:10.
GHOSTS BOOGIE ON AND CONTINUE THEIR DANCE.
MUSIC FADES AND STOPS AT 2:40.
GHOSTS BOW AND WITHDRAW.

Act IV

Scene 1   Advice from another age

VICTOR AND MIRA WALK ONTO STAGE TOGETHER

VICTOR	So what's the plan?
MIRA	No plan. First you fall in love and then I do, and then we see what happens.
VICTOR	Okay. Why me first?
MIRA	It's traditional.
VICTOR	Says who?
MIRA	I don't know. Look, Pish said you'd fall in love first and then I would.
VICTOR	When does it happen.
MIRA	Apparently you'll know when it happens.
VICTOR	Okay. Sounds like a good plan.
GHOST 3	(off stage) Wooooo! Wooooo!

GHOST 3 ENTERS

	Sounds like a terrible plan. Stop!
MIRA	No, you stop! Avaunt thee, ghost of Martin Heidegger!
VICTOR	Avaunt thee? And I don't think it's Marty.
GHOST 3	Aren't you the clever clogs?
VICTOR	It's Anne. Anne Hathaway.
MIRA	I love her films! She's so beautiful, but vulnerable, too, in an intelligent way, bemused by the complexities of modern life, but doing her best to work through them. And always learning something important about herself in the process.
VICTOR	Not that one. The other Anne Hath… I mean, the real Anne Hathaway.
MIRA	There was another one?
GHOST 3	Yes, you slops-slut, there was another one. And I'm her.

VICTOR	She was the wife of William Shakespeare.
MIRA	Wasn't he someone else?
VICTOR	No, he was real. As real as Les Murray.
MIRA	Les Murray—he wrote some beautiful things.
VICTOR	Yes, well, it's called the beautiful game.
GHOST 3	I'm here to advise you against this ridiculous plan of Pish's.
MIRA	Why?
GHOST 3	For a starter, it's the brainworm of Pish. That should be enough for you. But if you want more, then I'll give it to you.
	Love is for gulls.
VICTOR	Girls? Or the birds? Sea gulls?
GHOST 3	Gulls! You cloth-eared dolt!
VICTOR	You're the one with a sheet over your head.
GHOST 3	Hey! Don't diss Auslan.
MIRA	I thought it was Islam?
GHOST 3	No, Auslan, I think. Something about not communicating with the deaf after death or something. I don't know. I don't listen to them. Anyway, we've got to wear them.
MIRA	You were telling us about love.
GHOST 3	Yes, it's for gulls, for fools, for idiots who haven't got sense enough to look around them.
VICTOR	This is a surprising attitude from the wife of a man who wrote some of the most exquisite love poems in the world.
GHOST 3	To another.
MIRA	Yes, that might colour your opinion…
GHOST 3	It has nothing to do with that. Will loved me well enough, and I loved him. But we weren't stupid enough to fall in love with each other! That's for those who can afford it and those without brains enough to avoid it. And nothing else to do.

	He may not always have been immune to it, perhaps I wasn't either in my younger days. So what?
	You are here to do, not to feel, not to think, to do. Not to think about how you'd feel about thinking about doing something. To do. To build, acquire, achieve, to do.
	Love stops you doing. It's only feeling. It's only thinking, dreaming. It's a dream of life, not life. And life is all you have and that only briefly.
	Don't dream. Do.
VICTOR	Do what?
GHOST 3	Cretin! It doesn't matter *what*. DO!

GHOST 3 STORMS OFF STAGE

VICTOR	Falling in love might be doing something, mightn't it?

Scene 2   He falls for her

VICTOR AND MIRA REMAIN ON STAGE, LOOKING AT EACH OTHER

MIRA	Has that changed anything?
VICTOR	That hasn't changed anything, but everything has changed.
MIRA	What do you mean?
VICTOR	It's happened.
MIRA	What has?
VICTOR	Your words, your voice. When you speak, I can feel your voice vibrating inside me. It lights my body like glow-worms in a cave. I can feel a thousand points of light inside my body, glowing, warm, vibrating. Speak to me again!
MIRA	What should I say?
VICTOR	That!
MIRA	No one's ever really commented on my voice before.

VICTOR	Because they're all deaf. The sound of your voice is like drinking honey. Look! Look at my arm! My hairs are standing up trying to feel the air move with that voice. They want to touch it!
MIRA	(*STOKES HIS ARM*) Silly. You're probably just cold.
VICTOR	I'm burning. I can still feel your touch. Really. I can still feel your touch! It's as if you're still touching me. My skin is electrified. I can still feel you.
MIRA	(*LAUGHING*) Pish doesn't muck around when he wants to create an effect, does he?
VICTOR	(*STUDYING HER FACE*) You are so beautiful. I always knew you were beautiful. The first time I saw you, I saw you were beautiful, but now I can see the beauty itself. You are so beautiful, Mira. I keep wanting to touch you. You are so beautiful. It's exhausting. I can hardly breathe. Every one of my sense is overloaded. My skin still feels your touch. My eyes don't know where to look; everything, everywhere on your body, you are so beautiful. I just want to cry.
MIRA	Wow. It sounds wonderful.
VICTOR	Not as wonderful as you sound. And I've just noticed the way your lips move when you form words, when you make that tiny pause before you speak. Your lips are beautiful. They invite kissing.

VICTOR MOVES TO KISS HER.

MIRA	Whoa, Tiger! Slowly, slowly now.
VICTOR	Sorry. And not sorry. Your lips are so beautiful they are singing for a kiss. I could just watch them: the way they separate when you are about to speak. It invites intrusion. They invite kissing.
MIRA	What else do you feel?
VICTOR	My whole perception is accelerated and random. I perceive everything about you at once, in a whirl, as if your whole life, purpose, being, body, everything was laid bare before me in a single instance, and then without me knowing how or why, I see a single element of perfection: your

	voice, your lips, and now your skin. (*EXAMINING THE SKIN OF HER FOREARM*) Your skin is flawless.
MIRA	(*WITHDRAWING HER ARM*) My skin is not flawless. It's anything but flawless.
VICTOR	(*TAKING HER HAND AGAIN AND EXAMINING HER FOREARM*) Your skin is flawless. Flawlessly beautiful. (*SMELLS HER SKIN*) And perfumed. Perfumed like the petals of a flower. Not overpowering, not the flower itself, but the remembrance of a scent. It's intoxicating, but fleetingly intoxicating. It disappears. It's like a perfect hit of alcohol that leaves you sober! I want to drink your skin.
MIRA	If ever I need a stalker, Victor, you've got the gig!
VICTOR	Oh, please! Please! Let me stalk you. Let me follow you. Let me watch that perfect body sway its way away from me and let me follow. Tell me to go away and then relent and let me run to catch you. Then send me away again. And relent. Spin me round and round and let me feel that rush of always turning back to you.

Look at me, Mira. Let me drink in your eyes. |

Scene 3   She falls for him

VICTOR AND MIRA STAND, LOOKING INTO EACH OTHERS' EYES.

MIRA	Your eyes... Your eyes are beautiful.
VICTOR	My eyes are busy.
MIRA	Victor, your eyes are so deeply beautiful... I've never seen eyes like yours...

Oh, my God! It's happening...

I feel it, too... |
| VICTOR | What do you feel? |
| MIRA | I can feel your eyes inside my own. I can feel you exploring me. As your eyes explore me, I can *feel* it. I can feel the trail of your eyes over me! It feels wonderful, Victor. |

VICTOR	(*TAKING HER HAND*) I'm almost too happy to speak now.	
MIRA	I can feel you hand touching me inside my skin. Does that make any sense?	
VICTOR	No. Who cares?	
MIRA	I can feel your hand beneath my skin. It's like an extra pulse that's beating in response to my own. I can feel you inside me, Victor. I can feel your breath in my lungs, as if we were breathing with the same lungs, as if there were no separation between us.	
	I can feel you, Victor, as if you were seeping through my body, as if we were becoming mingled in the same body. How are you doing this?	
VICTOR	I don't know.	
MIRA	How can this be happening?	

THE FOLLOWING ACTION SHOULD BE SLOW AND BALLETIC. THEY STARE FIXEDLY AT EACH OTHER. THEY JOIN BOTH HANDS, BUT ARE STANDING A LITTLE APART. THEY LEAN IN TOWARDS EACH OTHER AND KISS, GENTLY, LIGHTLY. AS THEY KISS, THEY MOVE IN TOWARDS EACH OTHER AND THEIR ARMS MOVE TO ENCLOSE EACH OTHER. THEY PRESS THEIR BODIES TOGETHER, TURNING SLOWLY TO ENTWINE THEMSELVES CLOSER TOGETHER. THE KISS DEEPENS TO A SLOW AND SHUDDERING END AND THEY GAZE WORDLESSLY INTO EACH OTHERS' EYES.

Scene 4   Battle of the bands

VICTOR AND MIRA STAND, LOCKED IN EACH OTHERS' ARMS. SLOWLY, THEY BREAK APART.

VICTOR	Wow.
MIRA	Wow, indeed. Wow and double wow.
VICTOR	Did that just happen?
MIRA	It happened for me.
VICTOR	Me, too.
MIRA	Do you feel…

VICTOR	Yeah, I think so…
MIRA	Do you feel different again?
VICTOR	My head's still spinning.
MIRA	Changed again?
VICTOR	Not so…
MIRA	Connected…
VICTOR	Intense…
MIRA	But it was real, wasn't it?
VICTOR	Real for me, yes.

DISCORDANT JAZZ FADES IN. SPIRIT 3 JIVES ON.

SPIRIT 3	Yeah! Man, and now the come down. After a great gig, there's always the come down.
VICTOR	Who are you?
MIRA	Miles. He's the Spirit of the Keyboard. Musical keyboard. His name's a homage to Miles Davis.
VICTOR	Didn't he play the trumpet?
SPIRIT 3	Who cared what he played, man? He played!
MIRA	What are you doing here, Miles?
SPIRIT 3	I'm here to help you guys. You felt what it's like, now you've got to decide.
MIRA	Decide what?
SPIRIT 3	You've got to decide if you're going to fall in love or not.
VICTOR	Wasn't that it?
SPIRIT 3	That was a taste, man. A taste. That was, like, Track 1. There's a whole LP to come, man.
MIRA	What? What's an elpie?
SPIRIT 3	Love. Perhaps. You've had a taste. Pish offered it to you, but you have to accept it if you want it.
VICTOR	I want it. That was the most amazing experience of my life. I want that again. And again. And forever!
MIRA	It was good. But what's the catch, Miles?
SPIRIT 3	Catch, what catch? There's no catch.
MIRA	Except…

SPIRIT 3	Except that it isn't real. But I'm a spirit! Who cares about real? Ain't gonna trouble me, real or not.
VICTOR	It felt real to me. It was real. It was a real feeling. I feel it now. It's real.
MIRA	Really?
VICTOR	Well… I feel something. Something like I felt. I think I could feel it again. I'd like to feel it again.
MIRA	But what do you feel now?
VICTOR	Now? Now is an echo of the feeling, I suppose. But I want to feel it again. I love you. Could love you. And you could love me. You did for a moment there.
MIRA	For a moment, yes. But wasn't that just Pish?
VICTOR	Who cares? It was great! We might be made for each other, mightn't we? This might be meant to be!
GHOST 2	(*OFF STAGE*) Woooooo! Woooooo!

GHOST 2 ENTERS

	It isn't.
VICTOR	What do you mean it isn't? How do you know?
GHOST 2	Because I already told you, you have to engineer your destiny. There isn't any other kind. You engineer it, or it doesn't exist.
MIRA	Who's this?
VICTOR	Anne Hathaway. The other one. The actor.
MIRA	Really? Anne Hathaway? I love your films! I love you! You're my all-time favourite actor!
VICTOR	You love her? Five minutes ago, you loved me.
MIRA	Different love. But point taken. Sorry. What do you mean, Anne? About destiny, what did you tell Victor before?
GHOST 2	Destiny is an expression of will. It isn't something that happens to you. I made the films I made because I worked to make those films. It's not enough to be hard-working and talented.
VICTOR	And beautiful.

Act IV Scene 5 It isn't going to work

GHOST 2   And beautiful. You have to know what you want and you have to create it. Out of the nothing that the ghosts and spirits inhabit, you have to create it. That's what matters: the creation of it out of the nothing.

MIRA   But what is IT? What's the IT?

SPIRIT 3   IT is whatever it is, babe! Listen to Miles Davis. He's making it up. Making it up as he goes! And that's IT. That's the IT for Miles Davis. The IT for you, that's up to you.

GHOST 2   IT can be anything. Just not nothing. Don't choose nothing. Wooooooo!

Exit Ghost 2

SPIRIT 3   Catch you 'round, cats!

Exit Spirit 3

Scene 5   It isn't going to work

MIRA   Isn't Anne Hathaway still alive?

VICTOR   Not now. Not the now of the script, but the now of the performance, which is apparently two hundred years from script now.

MIRA   That's confusing.

VICTOR   You think that's confusing? Eight minutes ago, my entire body was alive with light, with an energy I've never felt before. And now, I'm talking to the woman I loved with the greatest love of the age as if she were serving me a sandwich.

MIRA   I'm sorry, Victor. I did love you. And I loved feeling love. It was a first for me.

VICTOR   Me too. Why does it feel as if love can't work now?

MIRA   Is now 2014 or 2214?

VICTOR   Doesn't matter. Can't work now, can't work then, can't work past, can't work present, can't work future. Love can't work. Can it?

MIRA   Are you going to keep coming to the gym?

VICTOR	Are you going to keep working here?
MIRA	Probably not.
VICTOR	Probably not, then. I would like to get fit, though.
MIRA	Why?
VICTOR	I'm not ready to die. Getting fit mightn't make me live forever, but it's my best shot. And I do want to live forever. And love forever. Love you or someone else. But I loved you first. I want to live or love forever. Like Les Murray. And not just in this play, but outside it. And if I do, you'll live forever, too. You could say, "I was his first love." And you would live forever. We can be great in the age of Pish without Pish. We could be like the great ones without being great ourselves. Like Heidegger or Anne Hathaway. They'll live forever.
MIRA	You have noticed that they're both dead, haven't you? All the great ones of any age, all dead.
VICTOR	If this is two hundred years from now, we're dead too. Long dead.
MIRA	Feels all right. All dead. Us, everyone. All dead. Feels all right.

VICTOR AND MIRA HOLD HANDS AND EXIT

Scene 6   Ghost Dance V

"YOU GOTTA GET UP AND DANCE" BEGINS FROM 0:00.

GHOSTS BOOGIE ON AND DANCE EXUBERANTLY.

AS THE SONG PROGRESSES, ALL OTHER ACTORS, STAGEHANDS, TECHNICIANS, DANCE ON AND JOIN THE DANCE.

ALL DANCE TO END AND INVITE AUDIENCE TO DANCE.

CURTAIN AT END OF SONG.

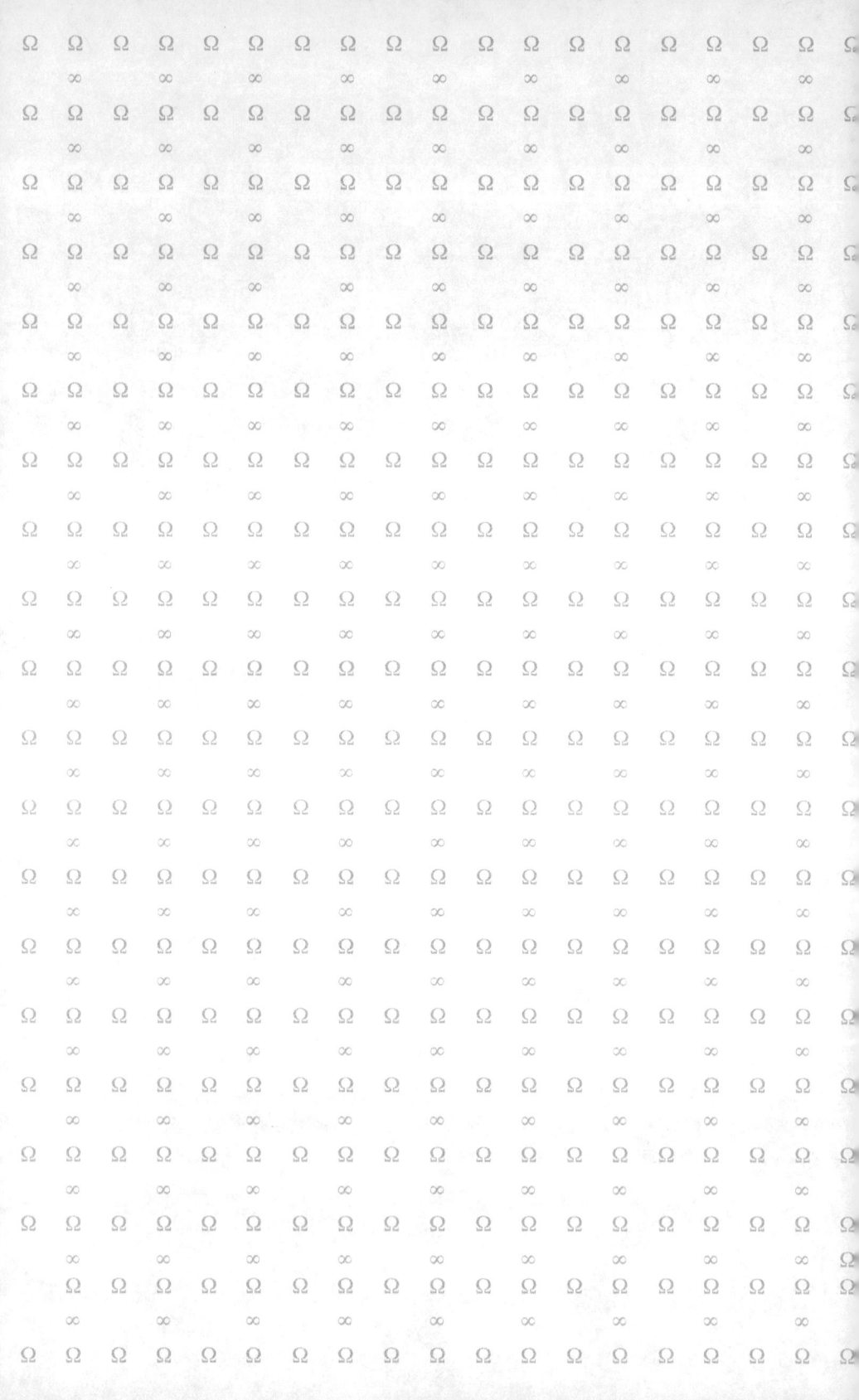

www.ingramcontent.com/pod-product-compliance
Lightning Source LLC
Chambersburg PA
CBHW032051290426
44110CB00012B/1049